THE HORSE SHOW
AT MIDNIGHT

. . . and yet if you ride confidently and well,

and ask confidently and soundly

for the horse's best level of performance,

his response will be to the ride you give him,

and not to your secret thoughts.

—WILLIAM STEINKRAUS

THE HORSE SHOW
AT MIDNIGHT

Poems by Henry Taylor

Louisiana State University Press/BATON ROUGE

7/1974
am. Lit

Acknowledgments

Some of these poems have appeared in *Plume & Sword, The University of Virginia Magazine, The Beloit Poetry Journal, Shenandoah, The Georgia Review, Stylus, The Chronicle of the Horse, The Sixties, Cargoes, The New Mexico Quarterly,* and *New Writing from Virginia.*

For help and guidance over the years during which these poems were written, I would like to express my deep gratitude to Fred Bornhauser, Richard H. W. Dillard, Eleanor Fletcher and The Noonday Bookshop, Walter Fletcher, George Garrett, Louis Rubin, May Sarton, and William Jay Smith.

PS
3570
A93
H6

ISBN 0-8071-0810-3
Library of Congress Catalog Card Number 66-17214
Copyright © 1966 by Louisiana State University Press
Manufactured in the United States of America
Designed by Robert L. Nance
1972 printing

CONTENTS

I

II

III

I

In Medias Res

I had a Latin master once
Whose name was J. B. Laramore.
One year we read of arms and men
And memorized the motto of
The University of Chicago:

Let knowledge grow from more to more
And so be human life enriched.
He also taught what he called *tact*—
Satiric, exaggerated respect
("Now when you get to be my age—"

"Almost old enough to vote, sir!")
For those whose age was so near ours
They might have been insulted by
Honest pretense at subservience.
He sat before us in the afternoon

And drummed into our memories
Vergil's verses, in small doses:
Perhaps someday thoughts of these things
Will bring us joy. "The tears at the heart
Of things . . ." interminable pause—

3

"*omnia migrant*: all things change."
The last day I saw him, he called
An early halt to the final exam,
And asked us all to leave.
Silently we filed beside his desk

While he gazed, speechless, at the window.
I did not see him at graduation.
I like to think he was afraid to come.
When I had my diploma in my hand,
I locked the door of a cinderblock room
And left love and my Latin book behind.

Three Snapshots/for George Garrett

1. A DEATH IN THE FAMILY

Ed Harrington came to the door
One time, and spoke to my father.
"You ain't got any old dark suit
You want to expose of, is you?
My wife's brother's wife
Has gone and joined the air crew."

"How did she die?" my father asked.
"Deed I don't know, Mister Tom.

4

She went down into the cellar
To get some fruit or somethin',
And just ceased down there."

2. BLACKBERRIES

On top of a ragged hill on the farm
Next to my father's, an old man
Sat on his front porch and reigned
Over a dominion of thistles and briars.

In his meadow, never mowed,
Blackberries grew wild, overran
The field, smothered the grass,
Bound the cows and ate them alive.

My sisters and I would steal
Under his fence, armed with pails,
To pick as many berries as we could.
We never got them all, although we tried.

One afternoon we stood in the briars
Reaching for berries over our heads,
Each one hanging before us like a bunch
Of grapes, when down from his porch

The old man tumbled, down the hill
Toward us, wild white hair in the wind,
Scattering all of his chickens as he ran.
His tiny dog yapped at his heels.

"Go back where you belong right now!"
And he waved his arms. We turned
And ran for the fence, clutching the pails
In our arms, scattering berries behind.

We looked back once and saw him on the hill,
Shaking his fist in the wind and shouting.
"If you're too lazy to raise your own
Blackberries, by God, you shan't have mine!"

3. MULE TRADER

Not long after the mule we'd had
For years had died, my father
Saw the man we'd bought it from.
He had a face so brown and hard
It would crack to pieces if he smiled.

"How's the finest mule I ever sold?"
My father told him the mule was dead.
"You, sir, are a God damn liar!
I been selling mules for forty years,
And I ain't never heard of one dying!"

The Stones of Emptiness

When Cortez came to Mexico,
Crawled, rushed, clambered, swept

Into the city of the Aztecs, he found
A tribe of handsome holy men
As ancient as the gods, who
Nursed, indulged, and fed
For a year their human sacrifices
To the hungry and inexorable
Tenants of their temple, then led
Them joyfully up the steps of stone
To the pinnacle of the pyramid.
There, in one small consecrated room,
Upon an altar like a slab, those boys
Lay down and let their hearts
Be taken as they lived and breathed.
Blood ran, fell, spurted from their
Wounds, and stained the walls
Until, after centuries had passed,
Huge scabs hung even from the ceiling.
Flutes as well as priests escorted
Those young and satiated boys
Up the heavy steps, and were broken
Before the temple's open doors.
But Cortez and his stainless soldiers
Stood in that Aztec city,
Above those brown and quiet men,
And commanded, with their long unwielded swords,
That these inhuman heathen rites must cease.

They feared to tear the temple down.

Now, among the crumbling Aztec temples
Wide women walk, with husbands
Bearing cameras and straw hats,
Their feet an ignorant and continual
Irreverent shuffle on the tile.
They look about from time to time, and nod,

And ask their guides how old the temple is.
The walls reverberate, and their questions
Echo back. The answer is the music
Of those shattered flutes, that hangs
Still on the musty air, a prayer
For those vanished civilized and holy men.

No blood runs down those cold stones now.

Over the River and Through the Woods

High in a house above a city
My grandmother has waited
For the last thirty years
With the sight going out of her eyes.

At last, it is whispered
By sisters and aunts
In tones of relieved condescension
That my mother's mother is dying
Because of a cancer in her blood.

My parents, who have never been
Her eyes, bestow on me the guilt

8

Of their neglect, and force me
To feel compelled to visit her.

Reluctantly, experimentally,
I walk into the room
Which she has darkly decorated
For the likes of me.

Fearful of bacteria, she
Will not let me take her hand,
But clasps her own two hands
In a gesture of greeting
And shakes them in the air.

For a little more than an hour
She tells me all the important things.
Daily, in front of a window,
She marches in place for exercise.

She has an ingrown toenail
Which her doctor forbids her to cut.
My sisters keep secrets from her,
She says, and the walls eavesdrop
On our conversation.

Gratefully, patiently she sits
As I take my leave,
Clasping her shaking hands,
Saying goodbye to the chair
I have been sitting in.

I am lowered down through the house
And I walk through the door
Out onto the street,
Back to my own more familiar
Decaying picture of things.

Remembering Kevan MacKenzie

Once upon a time I spent a summer
At a camp for children far from here,
Teaching riding to young boys and girls.
I taught them to make a horse go straight,
The way to make a horse stand still.
They grew and danced like weeds before my eyes.

Now there remains in my mind's eye
One face of all the faces of that summer;
It smiles at me, and I sit here
Wondering what's become of all the girls
That Kevan MacKenzie hounded straight
To earth, and may be chasing still.

Every week there was a dance, and still
I can recall the roll of those girls' eyes
As they hunted love, the first of summer:
Kevan, refusing to dance, stood straight
By the wall and dared the girls
To rout him from his sanctuary here.

Later he began to dress with care, and here
I remember the guarded gleam in his eye
As he came through the door and went straight
For the oldest and prettiest girl,
While with that stare that disturbs me still
The young girls hunted the first love of summer.

In the arms of that tall breath of summer
He danced, and looked her waist in the eye.
I whispered then, "Be cheerful, girls,
The sunshine boys are here."
When the music at last grew still,
The tall girl smiled, once more stood straight.

The days of dancing and love rode straight
To the last long week of that summer.
When I said goodbye to my boys and girls
I stood among them with tears in my eyes,
While Kevan MacKenzie, smiling still,
Said, "You must be glad to get out of here."

Now I sit here in another summer
And rising straight in my mind's eye
Kevan and his girls are dancing still.

For Mary Jay, Practicing Archery

Barefoot, armed to the teeth
With a forty-pound bow, dressed
In a two-piece bathing suit,
My sister marches forth against
Six numbered colored plastic circles.

Oh, she knows what the boys
Will say about this exercise,
How brazenly it gleams with hope
For the shape of things to come.
But as she stands before that

Target filled with straw, she sees
Those numbers on the hearts of men,
Dreams of soft-eyed deer and flying birds.
She takes good aim for the highest score.
She dreams her feet as fleet as Atalanta's

And wishes for the runner who will
Summon up the speed to master her.

The sun shines on her careful hair.
When they are gone, she goes and pulls
The arrows out with care between

Her fingers, then returns to the foul line,
Placing the arrows one by one
Into the quiver fringed with suede,
And the ancient huntress runs once more
Among those hard grey hills.

A Bargain at Half the Price/for *Steve Canty*

On a blasted heath in Maryland
There stands a livestock auction house
Where, every other Wednesday, men come
From miles around to buy and sell
Cheap saddles, swap lies and horses.
One night, I remember, they
Auctioned off one hundred plastic
Crucifixes, one at a time.

Riders in cowboy boots and red
T-shirts take the horses

Up the aisle and back, while
The auctioneer, known as Honest John,
Pries loose the bids and shouts them out.
"Sixty dollars! God damn it,
Gentlemen, let us pray!"
In the stands men drink big
Orange drinks and sit with girls
In tight blue slacks, with dyed black hair.

Once a month, from somewhere comes
A little man with a big trunk.
He stands in the center of the ring
And pulls out halters, buckets,
Reins, a saddle with one stirrup
("Here, gentlemen, we have a saddle
For a one-legged man!"), until
You think he has some magic power.

Someone has said that once a man
Walks through the doors of X's
Livestock Market, he is forever
Doomed. He may be right. I like
To think that while a man
Stands beneath that roof, God
Forgives him, automatically,
No matter what he says or does.

A Story for My Mother

One begins at an early age to know
The standard relationships—that fathers
Always have wives who have to be mothers.
The young think pairs, not broken halves; so
When my mother's thin, blind father began
To become known to us, we children had
To ask where his wife was, and hear she was dead.
We could never ask where she was again.
We learned to love the ones who had to hold
His elbow when he walked, who lived with him
And tried to help him push a way through life.
We played at Blind Man's Bluff till we were old
Enough to blush, wonder, and pity him
His dark and windy days without a wife.

Two things were told when my grandfather died.
I learned his wife was still alive, and why
No one had told us. Driving through the night, my
Father said she'd lost her mind, and I tried
To understand the ways some people hide.

So the time had come to tell us now, I
Knew, because the news would break. My mind's eye
Moved across the fine newsprint: "Survived
By his wife. . . ." I think of those words often.
She'd sat there, acknowledging no one's presence,
Weekly ignoring my grandfather. I find
I forget what I knew of his existence,
Think only of his lips sewn shut in the coffin,
And the way her presence has crowded my mind.

Three hours of an evening nap were gone
When the phone brought me lurching from my bed
To hear my father's quiet voice push down
Through miles and hours of sleep into my head
To let me know my grandmother had died
And that there would be services next day
If I could come. If not, he understood: he'd tried
To reach me earlier. I could not come away,
And turned to sleep and dreams of work not done,
And did not think of that phone call for what seemed
Like hours. Later, stung by snow-reflected sun,
I wondered if the call were real or dreamed.
If I fear to ask about her any more,
Mother, understand me: things are as they were.

The Female Graduate Student/for *Kelly Cherry*

Almost constantly, I find myself
Stumbling on a stairway
Or sugaring the saucer

Where I was quite sure the cup
Should have been. Oh, yes,
I still present papers

Of a highly professional nature,
Superficially. But no one
Really believes me:

I cannot get poetry published.
I would get out
Of this place,

Except, of course, for the lease,
And the things I have purchased
On time.

17

The Circus Rider's Departure/for May Sarton

For years, in one of three red rings,
Above my horse, with arms like wings,

Balanced on one leg or arm,
I have traced circles in sawdust,

Swung down to soft sawdust to turn
Handsprings beside my horse's hooves.

The silent crowds that gaze to learn
What spins my sequined, silver clothes

Have not seen through to hours that must
Be spent imagining true form—

In empty tents, in muffled rings,
Rehearsing nonexistent things,

Tricks to seem to know what no one knows.

II

I worked for years: at first, merely
Astride, my feet in the stirrups,

Then standing up, then each handspring
In turn, each trick built on the things

Mastered before. There always come
The next things to be mastered, some

Somersault or balanced attitude,
Some sleight of hand or foot or horse

Which has not been attempted yet.
The time comes when there is no more

To learn, except what is too hard,
Impossible except in thought, and so

There are no further tricks to learn.
The essence of deception now

Is making practiced, easy tricks
Difficult and not difficult,

So that those gazers wonder how
The thing is done, and wonder why

The same thing is too hard for them.
The trick itself comes thoughtlessly.

The trick becomes an act of mind:
Reveal some evidence of strain,
Conceal that which cannot be learned.

19

So this was where I stood tonight.
The mirror in my dressing room

Reflected clothes in perfect order,
And yet some nameless thing was missing.

I could not see what was not right,
And so I rode into the ring,

Standing on my cantering horse,
My arms outstretched, my practiced smile

Arrested in its proper place.
As my body and my horse revolved

Among the wickets I had placed,
The trick that could not be performed

Became itself inside my mind:
The faces in the chairs came clear,

Reflecting the light on my face.
Not now. I turned one last handspring,

Dismounted, bowed, and left the ring.
The feel of sawdust on my hand

Is pleasant, but I know it now.
The trick I do not dare perform

Unfolds, revolves in my mind's eye,
And I can see through it, beyond

Performing it, to further hours
Of work, a cycle without end:

Another trick begins to show its face.

IV

And now the crowds have all gone home,
Lighting the dark with their faces.

Out in the evening now, I see
The clowns moving through deepening dark

In overalls, with trunks and pails.
My horse breathes softly beside me.

Slow as steamshovels, elephants
Exhale their last tubs of water.

The spectators all have departed,
The tigers are back in their cages.

The great brown octopus shadow
Of tent is down and folded now.

A whistle blows. I stand and watch
The painted train move down the rails.

Darkness descends on this suburb;
I have ridden my last matinee.

Beneath no lights I take the reins,
And I place my foot in a stirrup.
Slowly, astride, I ride away.

21

II

Mr. James Dickey in Orbit

The darkness is closing around us
And the loudspeaker calls out the hours
In seconds of waiting.
High in my tower of steel and fuel
Which points to the stars,

Bravely phallic,
I lie strapped to my seat
In a spacesuit.

The instruments cluster around me.
I give each of them one final handshake.
I close my eyes when the time comes,
Nestling down in my long chair.
As the weight of my body presses

Down into me, the colors
Pass in front of my eyes,
The glorious purple of Heaven.

25

The thunder of engines enraged
Makes the tower quiver in terror.

I rise, I float from the ground,
Into the heavenly purple.
For the moment, there is nothing
But darkness.
But the rocket knows what it is doing,
And it bends its course in a circle.
I look through the electrical eyes
And I see my green earth below me.
I shout three green cheers for myself.

The black sky resounds with my joy.
The stars, incredibly bright,
Shine through the blackness toward me.
In the blue of my joy I salute them.
Re-entry into the earth's air
Begins after my third tour of the sky.

I start my brave plunge to the ocean,
Exulting in the thunder of sun,
Of engines no longer enraged,
But burnt out.
My happy comrades are waving

From the deck of the ship that awaits me.
I shout as I crash into the sea.
I feel the capsule slow down,
And bob back up to the surface.
Blackness closes around me.

I hear the voice of my captain
Come over the loudspeaker toward me.
The blastoff has been postponed again.
There is weather over the ocean.

I greet the sad face of my captain,
And I smile.
His sadness does not disturb me.
I climb down from my tower in triumph:
Tonight I have marched through the heavens.
I shout three green cheers for myself.

J. V. Cunningham Gets Hung Up
on a Dirty, of All Things, Joke

Love, I have lain awake by night
And tried to get the punch line right,

And tried to keep, with fierce intent,
A firm grasp of my instrument;

Though words are scarce and thought is thick
My flawless grammar is the trick

By which, though I am short of wit
And slow to make my couplets fit,

I shall explain, with love and luck,
Three Chinese sailors and a duck.

27

Howard Nemerov Experiences Another Statue

Approximately a month ago—
Perhaps it was last week—no,
I believe it was yesterday.
I don't quite remember, really.
Anyway, as I walked in the park,
A funny thing happened to me.

Stout, of course, and upon
A pedestal, naturally enough,
Stood a statue of someone.
There were people all over
The place, newsboys, lovers,
And a man selling nuts.

Nobody else seemed to notice
What the statue did then.
As I gazed on it, it became
Transfigured before my eyes,
And it did a thing that seemed
To me remarkable, perhaps obscene.

As I said, no one took any notice.
I am sorry about that, in a way,
Because now you may not wish
To believe me. But it did that,
Honest it did, and so I thought
I would tell you about it.

A Conversation Between a Man and a Woman Who Talk As If They Were, Respectively, Robert Creeley and Denise Levertov

HE: Woman came
            myself to woo
        and with her came
            my coming too.

SHE: Why must you always either
        make your mazing overtures
        or relate in undertones
            adventures in a tense
        so past? Which do you do?

HE: Fine,
            thank you

very much.
                    And you?

SHE: Not so hot
                        as it was
        even in monotonic shadows
                of mud huts
        in Mexico where not a thing was new
                    is love like this.

HE: In fact
            we move
        in act
            of love—

SHE: An act not simple,
                        not baroque,
        remarkable in its
                        eloquence,
        eloquent in its
                        remarkableness.

HE: Somehow, sweetheart,
            I suspect
        that you have changed
            the subject.

SHE: Here in this room of purple shadows,
        my bearded, hairy-handed friend,
        the little worlds of our red eyes revolve
        so certainly that neither you nor I
        can ever say for sure.

George Garrett Gets at the Root of the Matter

Once, walking in the woods,
I came to a clump of Jack-in-
the-Pulpits, dancing in the breeze,
shaken by the Spirit, shouting from
under their canopies Are You Saved.
I pulled one up. The root a bulb.

I cut a little piece of it with
my knife and tasted it. Lay
on my tongue like raw potato,
then, after a time, took fire, burned
my tongue as pepperoni never did
in Rome, or artillery fire in Trieste.

Let someone else decide why
such a root held down that
holy figure. All I know is,
I walked for miles before
I found a spring, and cold
clear water tasted good.

31

James Wright Is Depressed by the Death of the Horse that He Bought from Robert Bly

Never have I seen the sky more clear
Than in Montana. Birds with eyes
Inside my bones confuse this clarity.
I stand here in this Montana field
Remembering when things were as they were,
And watch the silent eyes of a horse
Which I recently bought from a friend.

Small creatures are talking among themselves
In the grass around my shoes.
I discover, to my surprise
(For lack of a better word),
That the horse did not belong to my friend
In the first place.

Alone, alone, I sink to my knees
In the grass by an ownerless horse
And weep for all students of Spanish.
Minnesota is what I meant to say,
And they may never know.

And Robert Bly Says Something, Too

I

I wake to find myself lying in an open field.
About my head the ends of grasses
Wave softly in the wind.

II

I raise my head and turn on my side
And see a horse's tail swishing at flies.
It is attached to the end of a horse.

III

In my way I love to consider things I love—
Oh, often even in summer in this kind of field
I think I should be covered up with snow!

III

III

Things Not Solved Though Tomorrow Came

—For whether lighted over ways that save
  Or lured from all repose,
  If he go on too far to find a grave,
  Mostly alone he goes.
                    —E. A. Robinson

There is silence in this blue car now.
My daughter and I have driven for hours
Through early morning, where we started,
High noon on the turnpike, where we stopped
To eat in a pink brick restaurant,
On through to afternoon, the hour when
The sun shines on the sides of golden things,
Until we are struck dumb by nearness to the end,
The long green shadows of her boarding school
Where we are bound, where we arrive at last.

We unload the car in several trips,
Carrying up the stairs to the third floor
Her clothes, her blankets, pennants, lamps,

37

Stuffed animals. The job at last is done.
She stands before me, smiling, as I lean
Against the car, my hand on my thick middle,
Trying not to sweat or gasp for breath.
It is time for me to leave. She kisses me
On the forehead.
                    "Goodbye, sweetheart," I say.
"We'll miss you. Hit the books. Write home some time."

She kisses me once more, then walks away.
I think of last year at this time,
Her first year here, when neither she
Nor I could keep tears back for long.
She walks across the dying, dark green grass,
Her brown hair, her mother's hair, shining
As it comes between my eyes and the sun.
Some friends of hers are waiting on the porch—
A tall boy smiles, and she begins
To line up love in the nick of time.

Autumn is descending on this hemisphere;
Leaves are turning now, in Pennsylvania.
The sun is shining on the sides of things,
And another summer has come to an end.
I climb into my car and turn for home—
I have far to go, and not much time.
My daughter's face is formed inside my mind
And I say to it,
                    "When you were born,
Light of my life, I could not in
My wildest dreams imagine you like this."
                *   *   *   *   *
I am alone in my blue car once more.
You are home safe, and I turn south
Trying to retain some sense of your presence

At my side, some sound, but all I hear
Is silence deeper than our speechlessness.
My mind turns slowly back through these
Brown leaves, to autumns of my childhood.

In the cellar, in a spacious crate,
I kept a lamb until it died.
My father gave me another, and I tried
To feed it clover blooms and bottled milk.
I fed it every morning, every night.
One winter Saturday I slept late;
When I awoke, the sun was high, shone
Through dead leaves of trees outside my window.
I rose and heated the bottle of milk,
Went down the stairs and stood on my toes
To lean over the side of the crate.
The lamb lay still, would not arise.
I stood there for what may have been an hour,
Staring down at those dull and dusty eyes,
And thought of rabbits I had kept out back
The year before, and how the babies bled
To death one night when a weasel
Got through a hole I had not patched that day.

Darkness comes upon me on the road.
Before I assail the windy turnpike
I have to stop for coffee, noise and light.
There is a diner up ahead, next to a motel
Which advertises Rest For Weary Bones.
Inside, the clock above the smoking grill
Says eight-fifteen. I take a booth beside
The window, and watch the highway wind away.
A young girl brings a menu and a glass
Of water and stands above me, pencil poised,

Moving in time to the jukebox music
Which I had not heard until I looked at her.

I order only coffee. As she turns
Away she winks and asks me if I'm tired.
Daughter, your feet upon the dying grass
Did not move as hers do, dancing on these tiles.

When she returns she slides into the booth
Across from me, searches for three jukebox tunes
To spend my quarter on, and, as she touches
My hand and smiles, I see through coffee steam
And smoke the eyes that looked through me at lunch
This afternoon;
            they tell me I have far
To go, but I have stopped for now.
                      She lifts
The little jar of cream which I had left
Untouched beside the sugar bowl, holds it
Before her face as if to offer me
A toast, then drinks it down in one small gulp.

She smiles, and we sit talking now about
Where I have been, where I am going, how
She likes her work and why she does it.
The things I say are of no consequence,
Regardless of the effort I have made.
I forget words as I speak them, only note
Her nod, her eyes, how hard it is for me
To keep my daughter's voice from drowning hers,
To keep the world beyond the foggy window
From moving through the dark outside until
The lines that hold me to it are cast off
At last, and I am left with nothing but
Her face, the things our fingers touch, words I forget . . .

40

Daughter, I speak to her of you, say you
Are beautiful, think to myself that you
Must never know how, when I speak,
Hers becomes the face whose eyes I praise.

Hours, cigarettes and cups of coffee pass
And find us sitting at this table still,
Her fingers touching mine.
                           The man behind
The counter tells us it is time to leave.
I notice, as he speaks to her, a tone
Not at all familiar, as if we both
Were customers. I rise and start to say
It's Been Nice Talking To You, but no words
Come. She finds her coat and brings it to me;
I help her into it as if I had
Done so a thousand times before,
And we depart, when I have paid the man
Behind the counter, arm in arm.

We stand still outside for a moment,
Until we can see each other in this dark.
I suppose she must be twenty-five or so.
Daughter, love, I say to you I see in her
Eyes a thing I have not seen in yours,
A thing no one I've loved has let me see
For years. We do not speak.
                           She gets into
My car while I walk across the road
To the office of the motel, speak to
Someone, pay him money, go out with the key.
Speechless in the car, we cross the road
Together; I get out with my raincoat,
Go around to the other side and take
Her by the elbow.

It is cold out here,
Perhaps for the first time, I tell myself,
This fall. At home, where lights have probably
Gone out, late treefrogs may be speaking still
By the pond at the end of the driveway.
You have unpacked your things and gone to bed,
Thinking perhaps of the tall boy who smiled
At you this afternoon,
                        and I stand here
With this strange waitress, thinking thoughts I have
Not thought for years and years—
                        How one must act
At times like this to keep the moment real,
Create a world out of thin air: to keep
Things going as they are supposed to go.
          *   *   *   *   *
Inside, attempts at speech in the dim light
Of the desk lamp, then silence as before.
She comes into my arms for a minute
Or two, then disengages me and sits
Along the bed's edge, lights two cigarettes,
And holds one out to me ambiguously:
Daring or inviting me to sit down.
I sit down close to her and take her hand;
We smoke in silence for a time.
                        Why did
You bring me here? I almost ask, but know
That her reply would sound the same.
                        She rises,
Then crosses to the desk, close to the light,
And starts to take her clothes off. I undo
My tie, then stop and look at her. Her white
Waitress's uniform, unbuttoned at
The front, slides slowly down over shoulders
And hangs about her hips.

42

                                    I have come far
To find this room, this creaking bed, this light
That plays such tricks upon my eyes and on
Her hands and hair;
                          I think at this moment
I shall be here forever while all things
Grow old around me, pass me in the dark,
And I shall lie tortured in this cavern
Until death, or madness, comes.
                                        But now,
Straight from a pile of clothes upon her feet
She rises, moves into my arms,
An island rising from the sea.
          *   *   *   *   *

Now I lie here on this dishevelled bed
Relaxing my tense muscles one by one.
Remembering an old consideration
Born of an old embarrassment, I try
To drift toward sleep without moving a hand
Or breathing too loudly. I fall closer
To sleep, but feel something stir in my brain
And recognize a shame from years ago,
Remembering how, at school, I stained my
Underwear behind locked doors, night after night.
Longer ago than that, I crouched at night
In bed on all fours, sitting on my feet,
And rocked back and forth singing to myself
Or dreaming of the time I would be free,
And fell, at last, forward on my face,
Put my thumb into my mouth, and fell asleep.

And at this moment, as I fall toward sleep
I sense in this tenseness in
My arm the effort to keep
My hand, my thumb, beside me.

*   *   *   *   *

I dream of rabbits the weasel killed,
Of lambs that died in my care.

    *   *   *   *   *

When I awake, I am sitting up in bed.
This girl is gone, whose eyes shone with some thing
I had not seen for years till now, whose voice
Moved in me even through dark clouds of sleep.
I try to bring her face before my eyes,
But all I can remember is the way
Her dress hung on her hips as she stood before me.
It is still dark outside, and still.
In the hundred miles ahead of dark
Turnpike, there will be time enough, time
To remember faces, in that roaring chill.

I lie down and light a fresh cigarette.
I roll over on my stomach and stretch,
Then drop the cigarette in one instant
Of the coldest dread, one moment so short
It could contain but one impression, to be thought
About forever after it.

                In that
Instant, a giant thing stood over me:
Its legs were at my shoulders, hips and feet,
Its heavy, shining wings clapped on its back;
I do solemnly swear I heard its breath,
And felt its rasping jaws above my neck.
Oh, daughter, darling, what can this thing be?
Can it have been so wrong that you loved me?

    *   *   *   *   *

I rise from bed and take the road once more. The car
Rolls through the darkness
    as a fierce beast runs through cold,
Extinguishing a whispered calling in my ear.

44

Of what is past, I only know what I am told—
I can no longer tell whose voice is in the air.
Headlights try for secrets the road will always hold:
There are things I have not seen
    though I have been to where they are.

One Summer Night

I lie and listen to thunder and rain
And gaze at lightning reflected
On the wet leaves of trees outside
Until, through the darkness, I hear
The voice of my son, and I rise
And go down the hall to his room.

The storm shines in through the window
And I see that his bed is empty.
I run down to the lawn and call
To my slender, pale-haired son,
And his voice comes down from above me.
He is standing on top of the house,

His arms held away from his sides,
Looking down at me and smiling.
I ask him to come down.
On the peak of the roof he turns
And raises his eyes to the sky.
Rain falls from his hair to his back.

Once more lightning flashes
As he flexes his knees and leaps
Upward, his arms close at his sides.
He tilts his head and raises his arms
And begins his back-dive to earth,
Eyes closed and hair windblown.

He slows down in front of my face,
Upside down before my eyes,
His arms overhead toward earth.
I ask him again to come down.
We are caught there together, immobile
In a flash of lightning which lasts forever

And I call to him time after time
But he is unable to answer.
Smiling, his blue eyes closed,
His arms overhead toward earth,
His blond hair waving like seaweed,
He hangs helpless and silent before me.

A Blind Man Locking His House

The tall clock in the hallway strikes
The half-hour chime:
Twelve-thirty. Now the hour has come
For footsteps in the dark, that like
To wander through this house from room to room.

My wife and I live here alone,
So my wife thinks;
But in the dark my dark eye blinks,
Down passageways of pure unknown
The hunter starts to stalk, and my heart sinks.

I rise and gird myself to face
This sounding house,
One hand stretched out against the blows
From chairs that will not stay in place,
From anarchy that sightlessness allows,

The other rummaging for keys
In my coat pocket.

At each door, as I pause to lock it,
Relentless blood assails my eyes
And drives them crazy: useless in their sockets,

They still roll upward in my head.
By force of will
I aim them downward: through this chill,
Pretending to look straight ahead,
I make the footsteps think I see, until

Between me and this heavy tread
At least one door
Is safely locked. From door to door
I pass, and learn I am misled:
There is no safe place for me any more.

To such thoughts does this presence tempt me
As floorboards creak
That I might drive myself to break
My heart at last, and find it empty,
Because some thing stalks me and will not speak.

The hallway clock clangs like my heart,
In time with feet
That flee, and press behind, and meet
At last, and all of this is part
Of all this house. My pitiful conceit

Breaks down, and I shall not escape.
Older than air
Or the stairway, he is somewhere
In dust and stone that saps all hope;
When I lie down that sound will still be there.

Time and again my wife has said
No one is there;

But in the weather of despair
As I climb up through dark to bed
I hear his step behind me on the stair.

A Dream of a Distant Land

Deep in a darkness many weeks old
I stand alone at the rail of my ship
Listening to the sounds to which
I have not yet become accustomed:
The pump of engines nudging the boat
Through the clear, cold, endless night;
The crack of icebergs that surround,
But do not bind me; and forever
The crash of water on a coast
Where seals on the rocks move slowly.
On the deck, now, I am alone,
Only thinking of you, waiting
Where thoughts of ice and whales
Are rarely more than amusements,
But I know that below me men watch
The hands of curious instruments tremble,
Hunting for the best course south

49

To the Arctic Circle, the open sea,
Back home to the Temperate Zones,
Where I played as a boy in the first
Cold winds of autumn among shocks
Of corn covered with frost, and walked
In the fields where my father's cattle
Lived. Through the open window
At night I could hear horses
Cantering across a field of stubble,
Steering around the shocks of corn
One night when they got out
Like polar bears cruising among
The icebergs as they swim beside
My ship in the clothing of life
Itself: claws, eyes, teeth and hair,
Salt water running in their veins
As it runs in yours and mine.
I think of you waiting for me
In this land where summer is short
Enough to force you to remember winter.
Through the veins of the bear,
In your brain and in mine,
The blood that knows will blunder
Its way from season into season,
As it sends the fish beneath me
Through the dark, like horses
Dodging frozen white shocks of corn
On a stubble sea, their senses
Of direction trembling like the hands
On the dials of careful instruments below
That guide me to you from breaking waves
Where seals on the rocks move slowly.

The Horse Show at Midnight

I. THE RIDER

Now, the showground is quiet.
The spectators all have departed.
Along the wall of the arena
The jumps are lying, collapsed.
The moon shines down on the grandstand
As I walk out across the ring
Alone, watching for what may not be here.
I take my place as a judge
In the center of the ring, waiting.
Asleep in their stables, the horses
Awaken to my thought-out call
And rise from the straw and walk
To the ring, silently and formally.
One after another they march
Around the ring, proudly, like men.
I stand on my toes and speak softly—
They all start to gallop at once
Noiselessly, weightlessly,

Their hoofs beating only within me.
Around the ring, faster and faster,
Their manes like flame in the moonlight,
They gallop in single file,
Halt as I think the command,
Then walk out of the ring
Into darkness, proudly and softly.
One horse only stays with me
Straining to hear a command
That I am unable to utter.
On a sign from someone unseen
The jumps rise up into place
By themselves, hugely and suddenly.
The horse kneels down on the grass
And rises up with a rider.
As I watch from my place as a judge
My heart and my bones leave my body
And are heart and bones of this rider.
As the horse flies over the fences
The horseman whose heart is the judge's
Makes no movement or sound,
But the horse knows what he must do
And he takes the fences one by one
Not touching the poles or the ground.
At the end of the course he halts
And the fences retreat to the ringside,
Then my horse and his rider are gone.
Alone in the grandstand's shadow
I call to him time after time
But only my bones fill my body.
The rider and horse do not answer.
I walk across to the gate
Looking back once more at the ring
Watching for sound or a movement
Left behind by one horse that I love.

The empty ring does not echo
And the horse has left no hoofprints.
In the moonlight, alone, I sink down
Kneeling in nothing but bones
And I call to my horse once again
But the ring and the grandstand are quiet.

II. THE HORSE

In the darkened stable I move in my sleep
And my hoof stirs the straw and wakes me.
I rise, breathing softly, inhaling
The moonlight outside like perfume,
Straining to hear the command
That moved my hoof in the straw.
In my huge, shining shape I stand
Listening, and I hear the calling again.
Through the locked door of my stall,
Obeying, I march to the show ring,
Beside horses I cannot see, but feel
As their hoofs shake the air around me.
I march to the sound of a heart
That beats somewhere just ahead of me.
In the ring I lead a parade
In a circle, galloping and galloping,
And I wait for a change in the heartbeat.
I halt, and the others march out,
And I sink to my knees on the grass
As a body gets up on my back
And the man in the ring disappears.
I rise to my feet once again
And look around me at fences
Which have sprung like trees from the ground.
My shape fills the air as I fly

Over boards, stone walls, and poles,
And the bones on my back do not move.
Still I move to the beat of a heart
That brought me out of the stable.
I stop when I clear the last fence,
And the bones dismount, and I march
From the ring to the sound of the heart.
Back in my stable I lie down
Wide-eyed, breathless and shining,
Still hearing within me the call
That brought me over the jumps.
This time I cannot obey:
This man is only partly a rider
And the rider in him is within me.
Helpless, grief-stricken, and alone,
He kneels out there in the moonlight
With only his bones for a body,
His heart singing deeply within
A shape that moves with new life.
I believe in the singing, and sleep.